WWI

Weapons of World War I

John Hamilton

VISIT US AT
WWW.ABDOPUB.COM

Published by ABDO & Daughters, an imprint of ABDO Publishing Company, 4940 Viking Drive, Suite 622, Edina, Minnesota 55435.

Printed in the United States.

Edited by Tamara L. Britton
Graphic Design: John Hamilton
Cover Design: Mighty Media
Photos and illustrations:
Corbis, p. 1, 7, 9, 11, 12, 13, 14, 15, 17, 18, 19, 25, 27, 28, 29
Mark Miller, p. 20-21, 23
National Archives, p. 4, 5, 6, 8, 10, 14, 16, 22, 23, 26, 27, 28, 29
Photos of the Great War, p. 8, 9, 24, 25
Povl Clausen, p. 11
Cover photo: Corbis

Library of Congress Cataloging-in-Publication Data

Hamilton, John, 1959-
Weapons of World War I / John Hamilton.
p. cm.—(World War I)
Includes index.
Summary: An introduction to the artillery, poison gas, guns, tanks, and U-boats and torpedoes used in World War I.
ISBN 1-57765-917-1
1. Military weapons—History—20th century—Juvenile literature. 2. World War, 1914-1918—Equipment and supplies—Juvenile literature. [1. Military weapons—History—20th century. 2. World War, 1914-1918—Equipment and supplies.] I. Title.

D522.7 .H353 2003
940.4'1—dc21

2002033291

Table of Contents

DREADNOUGHTS

BY THE TURN of the twentieth century, Germany began a plan to build a great navy. It wanted to challenge Great Britain for control of the seas. In response, the British designed and built a new class of warship to counter the German threat. In February 1906, Great Britain launched the HMS *Dreadnought*. It was a new design of battleship that made other warships on the seas obsolete.

The *Dreadnought* was a monster-sized battleship. It could reach speeds of 21 knots (39 km/hr), and had armor plating 11 inches (28 cm) thick. It was armed with 10 12-inch (30-cm)

Below: The First and Second Battleship Squadrons of the German navy, in Kiel Harbor, Germany
Right: A diagram of the German *Dreadnought*-class battleship SMS *Nassau*

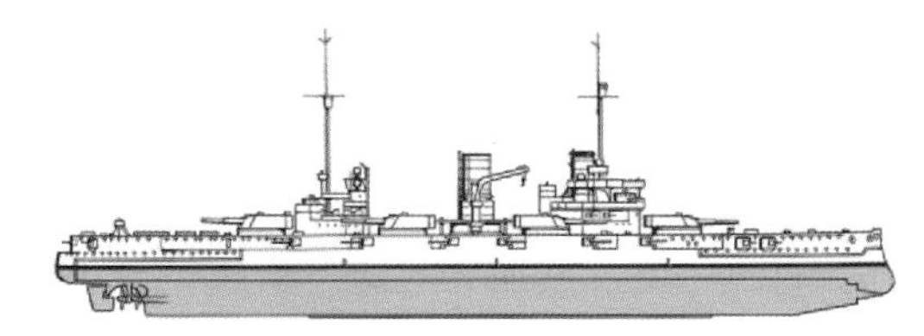

Left: The HMS *Dreadnought*, the British warship that revolutionized battleship design in the years leading to World War I

guns. These huge weapons could shoot projectiles 12 inches (30 cm) in diameter. Later *Dreadnought*-class ships also had many smaller guns for attacking the enemy's light forces at closer ranges.

All the major powers rushed to build their own *Dreadnought*-class battleships. This naval arms race added to the tension that eventually led to the start of World War I.

Left: A side view of the British battleship HMS *Dreadnought*.

ARTILLERY

ARTILLERY ARE BIG GUNS that can fire explosives a great distance. In World War I—especially on the Western Front, with its maze of trenches—artillery was used heavily in an attempt to break the stalemate. Each side used artillery to kill enemy troops in the trenches, to knock out communications lines, and to destroy enemy artillery units.

Artillery bombardments could last a long time, turning the countryside into barren, muddy fields of death and destruction. Creeping barrages rained curtains of shells down on the enemy just before infantry troops made their attack.

There were many kinds of artillery used in World War I, from light, horse-drawn field guns, to howitzers, to the German Paris Guns that were so big they had to be moved on railway lines. The most famous gun was Big Bertha, which could fire shells up to a distance of 70 miles (113 km).

Below: A German arms factory
Bottom: A British artillery battery fires at the German trench lines in France.

Artillery shells came in many varieties. They were measured by weight or diameter. Some exploded on impact, while others burst in the air, raining down deadly shrapnel on men in the trenches.

Troops with skilled ears could identify the type of artillery shells being fired at them from the sound the shells made while traveling through the air. Some shells cracked like golf balls being struck, others sounded like newspapers being torn in two. The most frightening ones shrieked across the sky and landed with deafening explosions. Artillery killed and wounded millions of soldiers. Even those who survived were affected. The heavy bombardments struck fear into the men in the trenches, causing mental illness in many.

Above right: A French soldier aims an “air torpedo” at enemy troops.
Above: The German “Big Bertha” terrorized the citizens of Paris, France.

MACHINE GUNS

MACHINE GUNS came to symbolize fighting in World War I, especially in the trenches. Machine guns were extremely effective automatic weapons. Most of the European generals at the beginning of World War I thought that massing their troops and charging forward would win battles. That was how wars had been fought in the past.

During World War I, however, the new technology of defensive weapons made this type of offensive plan obsolete. On the first day of the Battle of the Somme in July 1916, British forces suffered 60,000 casualties. Most of them were mowed down by machine guns when the British charged in large groups toward German lines.

The first automatic machine gun was the Maxim, invented in 1884 by Hiram Maxim in the United States. When a bullet is fired from a gun, compressed gasses produce a recoil effect, which jerks the weapon backward. Machine guns use the energy in the

Below: Hiram Maxim with his machine gun
Bottom: An American machine gun crew in France

recoil to automatically move the next bullet into the firing chamber. As long as the trigger is pressed, the gun keeps firing, sometimes as many as 600 bullets per minute. In the face of such withering fire, advancing troops out in the open had almost no chance of survival.

A group of machine gunners in a German trench prepare to fire their weapons.

The German army quickly saw the battlefield potential of the machine gun and copied the Maxim. They used machine guns in great numbers, even at the beginning of the war. The British and French were slower to incorporate them into their armies. But it didn't take long for all sides to recognize the importance of machine guns, and soon weapons factories all over Europe produced variations of the Maxim in large numbers.

The Germans called their version of the Maxim the MG 08. The British had their own variation, called the Vickers Gun. In the United States the preferred machine gun was the .30-inch Browning, which was similar to the Vickers Gun.

The machine guns used in World War I were heavy and cumbersome. It took a crew of men to operate them. They also produced a lot of heat when fired continuously, which made them stop working. But their firepower more than made up for their disadvantages. Machine guns killed millions of soldiers in World War I.

A British Vickers machine gun crew takes cover between two trees as it sets up to fire on the enemy.

U.S. troops train with Springfield rifles fitted with bayonets.

PERSONAL FIREARMS

WORLD WAR I saw the advancement of many technological developments on the battlefield, including machine guns, tanks, and poison gas. But it was the trusty rifle that most soldiers carried. Personal firearms were relatively light, dependable, and could be fired over and over again, as long as there was ammunition. Rifles were used both as defensive and offensive weapons.

In the years before the war started, several improvements were made in rifle technology. Instead of being single-shot weapons, the new rifles were reloaded with a bolt that was pulled back. Multiple shots could be fired using spring-loaded clips that held several bullets.

During World War I many types of rifles were produced. Several models, however, became very widely used. In Germany, the most common rifle was the 7.92mm Mauser Gewehr 98, usually simply called a Mauser. It had a superior design that made it dependable and accurate. It used a detachable clip system that saved time when reloading, which was crucial in battle.

Great Britain made extensive use of the Lee-Enfield .303-inch rifle. Nearly every British soldier on the Western Front received this rifle. Its magazine held 10 cartridges. It could be shot rapidly and accurately. With the right training, a soldier could fire up to 12 shots per minute. The Lee-Enfield was so reliable that it was used even through World War II.

The standard rifle of U.S. forces in World War I was the Springfield, which was produced in a short-barreled carbine version for the war. The Springfield was a reliable weapon comparable to the British Lee-Enfield. It was also produced in an automatic Mk1 version.

During World War I most soldiers used rifles in battle. Snipers also used rifles, sometimes with special optical sighting mechanisms to help in aiming. A sniper's job was to pick off the enemy from a long distance. Soldiers were warned not to stick their heads up above the lip of their trenches for fear of being hit by a well-aimed shot from a sniper's rifle.

However, in some cases, rifles were impractical. Soldiers in tanks were issued pistols. These weapons were easier to maneuver in a tank's cramped quarters. Officers and military police also typically carried pistols.

Above: Hans Clausen, a Danish soldier, poses with a Mauser rifle. Many Danes were forced to fight for Germany in World War I. Clausen fought from 1914 until just three months before the war ended in 1918. He was buried in a cemetery in France near the Somme River.

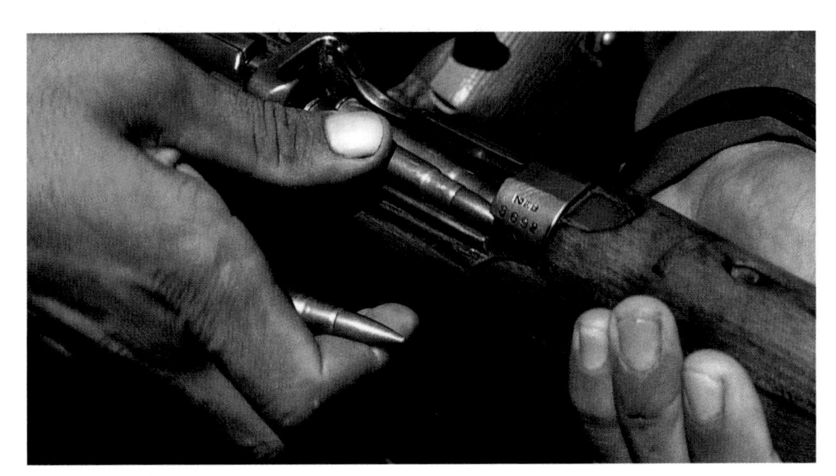

Left: A British soldier loads a Lee-Enfield rifle.

A recruitment poster urges troops to join the U.S. Tank Corps.

TANKS

WORLD WAR I saw the first use of the tank on the battlefield. The development of the tank was a big technological leap that would eventually help the Allied forces crack the stalemate of trench warfare.

The British were the first to invent tanks. But when early versions were tested at the turn of the century, the British saw little use for them in war. Lord Horatio Kitchener, who later became Great Britain's minister of war, called the tank "a pretty mechanical toy."

As the two sides of World War I settled into trench warfare on the Western Front, millions of troops died with little to show for their sacrifice. New attention was turned to the tank as a way to break the standoff. Winston Churchill, who became the British prime minister in 1940, formed the Landships Committee in 1915 to develop more reliable and battle-ready tanks.

Winston Churchill

British Mark I tanks were armed with two large guns and four machine guns.

A British tank goes over a trench. Tanks were sometimes called "Winston's Folly," but proved to be breakthrough weapons at the Battle of Cambrai in 1917.

The first tank used in battle was the heavy British Mark I, in 1916. Eighteen of these tanks took part in the Battle of the Somme on September 15. The Mark I had two large guns and four machine guns, and weighed approximately 28 tons (25 metric tons).

In 1917, at the Battle of Cambrai, tanks were used to flatten barbed wire from the battlefield and to clear enemy trenches. They also acted as shields for advancing infantry troops. Over 10,000 German troops were captured. It was the first coordinated use of tanks in battle that was considered a major success.

French Renault tanks were sometimes used by American troops during the war.

Early tanks often broke down or became stuck in muddy trenches. Conditions inside the tanks were almost unbearable. Several men were needed to operate each tank. They suffered through extreme heat and noxious fumes in the cramped interior.

As the war progressed, tanks became more and more capable and sophisticated. The British Mark V was used in combat in July 1918. The Mark V had a complex set of gears and brakes that allowed a single driver to operate it.

The French quickly saw the value of tanks and began mass producing their own designs. The United States also produced limited numbers of tanks, based on the lightweight French Renault design. The Germans were slow to embrace tank technology. They produced only 20 A7V 33-ton (30-metric ton) tanks during World War I.

A British tank tears through a barbed wire fence in no-man's-land.

Tanks support a U.S. infantry charge against a German trench in 1918.

POISON GAS

WHEN THE ARMIES of World War I found themselves stuck in the trenches of the Western Front, they tried desperately to come up with new ways of fighting to break the deadlock. One of these was the use of poison gas. The French were the first to use gas. During August 1914, they used tear gas against German troops. It was the Germans, however, who first used lethal gas on a large scale.

On April 22, 1915, French troops near the town of Ypres, Belgium, saw a yellow cloud drifting toward them from the German lines. They were shocked to discover the cloud was chlorine gas. Within seconds of inhaling the gas, the unprotected troops started choking uncontrollably. The men panicked and fled in confusion. But the Germans, who were surprised at the gas's effectiveness, didn't take full advantage of the break in the Allies' lines.

The use of chemical warfare brought immediate outrage from the rest of the world. The gas attack damaged Germany's relations with the neutral countries, including the United States. Soon, however, the Allies used gas against the Germans. By the end of the war, the Germans had released about 68,000 tons (61,688 metric tons) of gas, while the British and French unleashed 51,000 tons (46,266 metric tons). But instead of breaking the stalemate of trench warfare, the use of poison gas only added to the misery and horror.

Left: Gas masks were sometimes fitted on horses near the front lines.
Right: Two soldiers repair a telephone line during a gas attack.

A German machine gun crew fires on the enemy during a gas attack.

There were several kinds of gas used in World War I. The most common were chlorine and phosgene, which caused choking and lung damage, and mustard gas, which caused severe burning and blistering of the skin. The gasses also caused blindness, sometimes permanently.

When poison gas was first used in the war, it was released from large canisters along the trench lines when the wind was blowing toward the enemy. Sometimes, however, the winds shifted, and the gas drifted back over the attackers. To solve this problem, special artillery shells were invented to carry liquid chemicals that evaporated on impact, creating lethal clouds of poison gas.

The soldiers' only protection was to wear goggles and crude gas masks, which often didn't work. Toward the end of the war, filter respirators were available that used charcoal and antidote chemicals. These were very effective in keeping the troops safe from gas attacks, but were bulky and difficult to use in the cramped space of the trenches.

Poison gas was also used on the Eastern Front. The Russians were hardest hit by chemical warfare, suffering nearly a half million casualties. Approximately 56,000 died.

After the war, an outraged world banned the wartime use of poison gas in 1925. Most countries have stuck to the ban, although some keep stockpiles of gas for what they claim are defensive purposes.

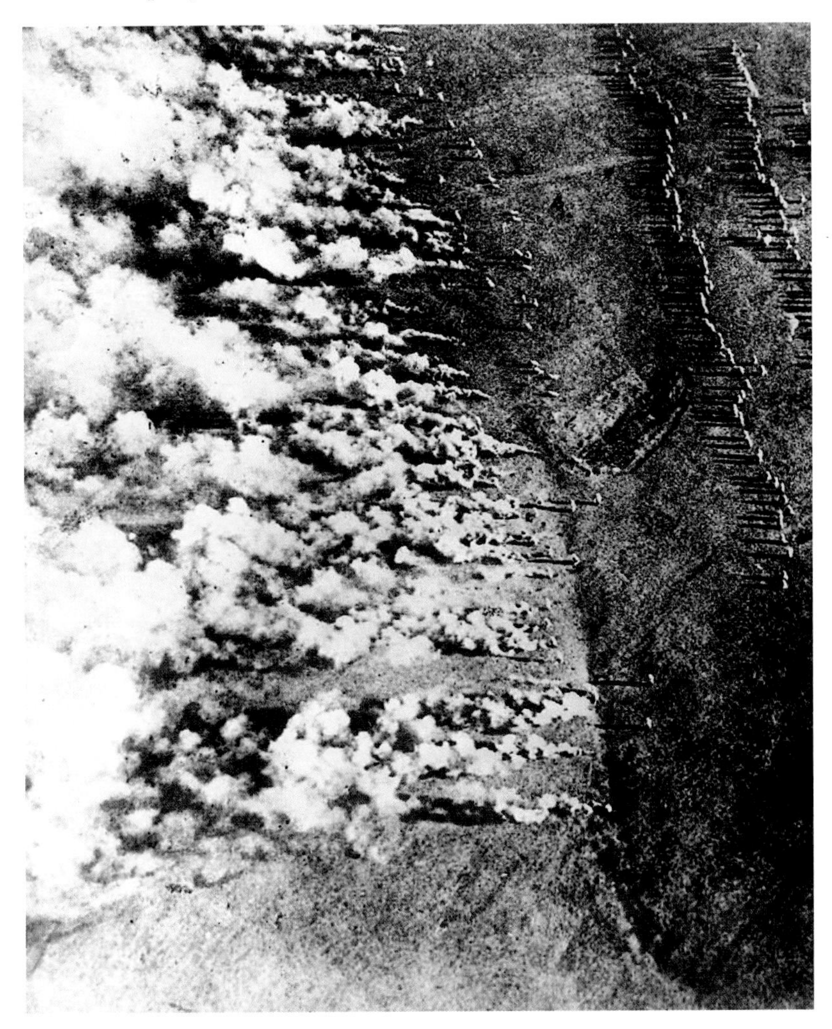

An airplane pilot's view of a German gas attack on the Eastern Front.

AIRPLANES

WHEN WORLD WAR I began in 1914, airplanes were a new invention. The Wright brothers had flown the first airplane just a few years earlier, in 1903. Some military leaders didn't think airplanes would have much practical use on the battlefield. Others, however, quickly saw their potential and started developing planes for use during war.

The first airplanes used in World War I were fragile craft that looked like apple crates with wings. They were slow, underpowered, and unarmed. As the war progressed, these early planes were replaced with powerful craft that were armed with advanced weaponry.

At the beginning of the war, bombs were dropped over the side of airplanes, and were very inaccurate. Later, special bomber aircraft were invented, with bombsights for aiming, and larger bombs that were held in racks beneath the airplane.

There were many different kinds of airplanes produced. Most were biplanes, with two sets of wings and a large engine mounted in the front. For extra lift and maneuverability, some airplanes even had three sets of wings. These were called triplanes. Germany's famous ace pilot, Baron Manfred von Richthofen, the Red Baron, at one time flew a Fokker Dr. I triplane, painted blood red.

The most feared German plane of the war was the Fokker DVII, which first flew in April 1918. It was easy to fly, quick, and rugged. Pilots could easily fly straight up, with guns firing, for a long distance without worrying about the airplane stalling. On the Allied side, the best planes of the war included the Sopwith Camel, the Sopwith Pup, the Nieuport 17, and the Spad XIII.

During the first part of World War I, airplanes were used for reconnaissance. Pilots could spot the enemy from the safety of the skies, and then tell artillery operators where to fire their shells. Eventually airplanes were used to drop bombs on the enemy. At first, pilots dropped bombs over the side of their airplanes by hand. Soon planes were fitted with bombsights and racks under the fuselage, which made striking the targets much easier. Pilots also learned to strafe, or shoot, troops on the ground with machine guns mounted on the airplanes.

Troops in the trenches were highly vulnerable to attack from the air. They tried shooting their guns at the airplanes, but the swift-moving targets were hard to hit. Both sides started sending up airplanes with the purpose of shooting down the other side's airplanes. These were specialized planes called fighters. Aerial dogfights became a common sight over the battlefield as pilots, sometimes called Winged Knights, tried to outmaneuver and outshoot each other.

Above: A German C.L. III A is brought down near the Argonne Forest by American machine gun fire. *Below:* Many aviators considered the British Sopwith Camel one of the best planes of World War I.

ZEPPELINS

A Zeppelin, accompanied by two German biplanes, soars over the countryside.

GERMAN AIRSHIPS first attacked Great Britain in the spring of 1915. The Germans wanted to disrupt production in enemy war factories. But the British lived on an island. They could see enemy attack ships coming from across the sea. The Germans knew they would need to attack the British from the air. To accomplish this, the Germans used Zeppelins, which were huge, slow-moving airships with rigid, internal frames.

Invented in 1900 by Count Ferdinand von Zeppelin, the airships were filled with highly flammable hydrogen gas. At the beginning of the war, Zeppelins could fly higher than airplanes, so they didn't have to worry about being shot down. They crossed the English Channel on calm, moonlit nights and dropped bombs on British targets, including England's capital, London. In all, there were more than 50 Zeppelin raids on Great Britain. Approximately 557 people were killed, and another 1,358 were wounded.

Although Zeppelins played a relatively minor role in the outcome of the war, they terrorized many British people. Many people had never even seen an airplane before. The sight of a giant Zeppelin lumbering across the night sky and dropping bombs on cities caused great panic.

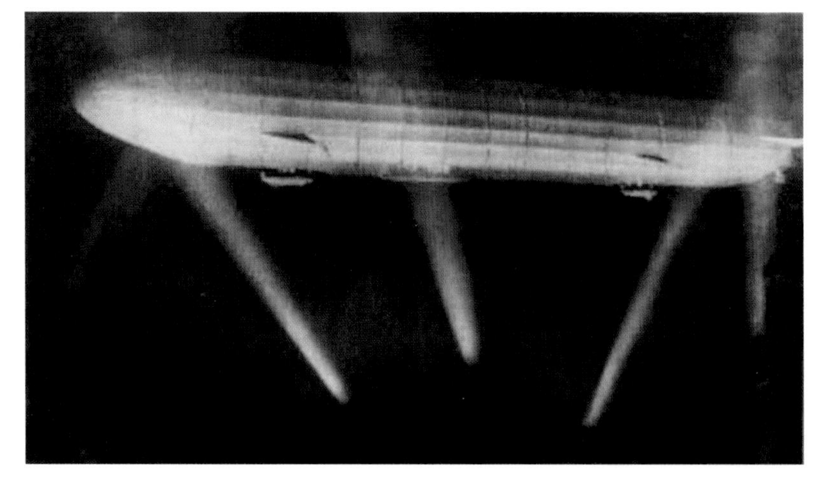

This photograph, which was probably staged, shows a German Zeppelin during a nighttime bombing raid over London.

A Zeppelin cruises over warships in Kiel Harbor, Germany.

In the later years of the war, airplanes developed more power and lift, and were able to fly as high as the Zeppelins. By using incendiary bullets, aircraft were able to ignite the Zeppelins' hydrogen gas. The huge flaming airships could be seen for miles away as they slowly fell from the night sky. In the last years of the war airships were mainly used as observation platforms to direct artillery fire on enemy troops. They were also used to spot enemy submarines.

An airship goes down in flames after tangling with a biplane over the English Channel.

A German U-boat surfaces in stormy seas.

U-BOATS

SUBMARINES FIRST SAW COMBAT during the American Civil War, but it was during World War I that they were used extensively. Germany wanted to choke off Britain's supply lines and knock it out of the war. They used submarines to attack convoys of merchant ships in the hope that Britain would run critically low on necessities such as food and ammunition.

By the end of 1914, the German navy kept most of its surface fleet close to home waters. It was afraid that Britain would launch an invasion across the English Channel. To attack the shipping convoys, the Germans relied on their U-boat fleet. U-boat stands for *Unterseeboot*, which is German for "undersea boat."

World War I-era U-boats were small compared to today's submarines. They carried a crew of 22 to 36 men. The space inside was cramped and stuffy. Fumes from the ships' gas or diesel motors polluted the air. When traveling underwater, U-boats used electric motors and batteries because their diesel motors needed air to run.

Survivors escape a ship sunk by a German U-boat.

While underwater, U-boats could attack enemy ships with torpedoes. While on the surface, they attacked with

deck-mounted cannons. German submarines did a lot of damage to Allied ships. During the course of the war, U-boats sank 5,554 merchant ships, plus many warships.

German submarines also attacked unarmed passenger ships. On May 7, 1915, a U-boat attacked the *Lusitania* as it passed close to Ireland. The ship sank, killing 1,198 people, including 128 Americans. The sinking of the *Lusitania* pushed an outraged America closer to joining the war.

To counter the U-boat threat, the Allies started grouping merchant ships into convoys, which were escorted by heavily armed warships. Airships were sent high above to spot the enemy submarines, and depth charges were dropped to try to destroy them. U-boat captains also had to worry about underwater mines. Life aboard a U-boat was very hazardous. The German navy built a total fleet of 372 submarines. During the course of the war, the Allies destroyed almost half, 178 in all.

Above: A line of submarines rests on the surface in Kiel Harbor, Germany, in 1918. *Below:* Sailors work inside the cramped quarters of a German U-boat.

Timeline

1906 *February:* HMS *Dreadnought* is launched by Great Britain, beginning a worldwide naval arms race.

1914 *June 28:* Austria-Hungary's Archduke Franz Ferdinand is assassinated by a Serbian nationalist while touring Sarajevo, the capital of Bosnia-Herzegovina.

1914 *August:* World War I begins as German armed forces invade Belgium and France. Most of Europe, including Great Britain and Russia, soon enters the war.

1914 *August 26-31:* Russia suffers a major defeat at the Battle of Tannenberg.

1914 *September 9-14:* Second massive Russian defeat, this time at the Battle of the Masurian Lakes.

1915 Turkish forces slaughter ethnic Armenians living within the Ottoman Empire. The Turkish government accuses the Armenians of helping the Russians. Casualty totals vary widely, with estimates between 800,000 and 2 million Armenians killed.

1915 *Spring:* German Zeppelins launch bombing raids over English cities.

1915 *April 22:* Germans are first to use lethal poison gas on a large scale during the Battle of Ypres.

1915 *May 7:* A German U-boat sinks the unarmed British passenger liner *Lusitania*, killing 1,198 people, including 128 Americans. The American public is outraged, but President Wilson manages to keep the United States neutral.

1916 *February 21-December 18:* Battle of Verdun. Nearly one million soldiers are killed or wounded.

1916 *June 24-November 13:* The Battle of the Somme costs approximately 1.25 million casualties. On the first day of the infantry attack, July 1, British forces suffered a staggering 60,000 casualties, including 20,000 dead, the largest single-day casualty total in British military history. Many troops are killed by a new battlefield weapon, the machine gun.

1917 *January 31:* Germany declares unrestricted submarine warfare, outraging the American public.

1917 *March 12:* The Russian Revolution overthrows Tsar Nicholas II.

1917 *April 6:* The United States declares war on Germany.

1917 *November:* Tanks are used for the first time on a large scale at the Battle of Cambrai. And on November 7, Russia is taken over by Lenin's communist government during the Bolshevik Revolution.

1917 *December 15:* Russia's Bolshevik government agrees to a separate peace with Germany, taking Russia out of the war.

1918 *March 21-July 19:* Germany mounts five "Ludendorff offensives" against strengthening Allied forces. The attacks are costly to both sides, but Germany fails to crush the Allied armies.

1918 *May 30-June 17:* American forces are successful against the Germans at Chateau-Thierry and Belleau Woods.

1918 *September 26-November 11:* French and American forces launch the successful Meuse-Argonne Offensive.

1918 *September 27-October 17:* British forces break through the Hindenburg Line in several places.

1918 *November 11:* Armistice Day. Fighting stops at 11:00 A.M.

1919 *May 7-June 28:* The Treaty of Versailles is written and signed.

GLOSSARY

ARMISTICE
A formal truce, or cease-fire, during which a peace treaty is decided on and signed by countries fighting a war.

AUTOMATIC WEAPON
A type of firearm that uses the force of the explosion of a shell to eject the empty cartridge case, put the next shell in position, and then fire it. This sequence continues as long as the trigger is pressed. A machine gun is an example of an automatic weapon.

BATTLESHIP
A large warship fitted with thick plates of armor and big guns. Just before the start of World War I, Great Britain launched the *Dreadnought* class, which made older battleships obsolete. By World War II, battleships became less important as aircraft carriers dominated the seas.

BIPLANE
A plane that has two sets of wings, one on top of the other. This was a common design of airplanes in World War I. Other designs included monoplanes that had a single set of wings, and triplanes that had three sets of wings.

CASUALTY
Soldiers killed or wounded in battle.

CREEPING BARRAGE
Also called a rolling barrage. Just before the infantry charged enemy trench lines, artillery sometimes laid down a creeping barrage, a steady curtain of bombs that slowly moved forward. In theory, the creeping barrage would clear the way for advancing infantry troops. In practice, however, the barrages could be poorly timed and inaccurate. Extended artillery fire often did nothing more than alert the enemy to an impending infantry charge across no-man's-land.

DOGFIGHT
Air-to-air combat between opposing sides of aircraft.

HOWITZER
A short cannon that delivers its explosive shell in a high arch. Howitzers are useful for lobbing bombs when the enemy is relatively close, such as in an opposing trench position.

INCENDIARY SHELLS
Shells that are designed to start fires on impact. They are often loaded with flammable material, such as phosphorous. Airplanes often used incendiary shells against Zeppelins in order to set them on fire and force them down.

NEUTRAL COUNTRY
A country that doesn't participate in a war between other countries. Sometimes neutral countries bend the definition of the word. Even though the United States stayed neutral until 1917, it actively traded goods and weapons with both sides, although it had especially close economic ties with the Allied countries.

NO-MAN'S-LAND
The area of land between two opposing lines of trenches.

OVER THE TOP
When one side advances out of the shelter of the trenches into no-man's-land and attacks the enemy.

RECONNAISSANCE
To explore or scout the enemy's position. Aircraft in World War I were very useful in discovering the enemy's exact location, which helped make artillery fire more accurate. As both sides began to realize the importance of aerial reconnaissance, they each developed fighter aircraft to shoot down enemy reconnaissance planes.

WEB SITES

Would you like to learn more about the weapons of World War I? Please visit **www.abdopub.com** to find up-to-date Web site links. These links are routinely monitored and updated to provide the most current information available.

INDEX